EMMANUEL JOSEPH

The Clockwork of Civilization, How History, Technology, and Philosophy Shape Human Progress

Copyright © 2025 by Emmanuel Joseph

All rights reserved. No part of this publication may be reproduced, stored or transmitted in any form or by any means, electronic, mechanical, photocopying, recording, scanning, or otherwise without written permission from the publisher. It is illegal to copy this book, post it to a website, or distribute it by any other means without permission.

First edition

This book was professionally typeset on Reedsy.
Find out more at reedsy.com

Contents

1. Chapter 1: The Dawn of Civilization — 1
2. Chapter 2: The Age of Empires — 3
3. Chapter 3: The Middle Ages — 5
4. Chapter 4: The Renaissance — 7
5. Chapter 5: The Age of Exploration — 9
6. Chapter 6: The Scientific Revolution — 11
7. Chapter 7: The Enlightenment — 13
8. Chapter 8: The Industrial Revolution — 15
9. Chapter 9: The Modern Era — 17
10. Chapter 10: The Digital Age — 19
11. Chapter 11: The Globalized World — 21
12. Chapter 12: The Knowledge Economy — 23
13. Chapter 13: The Anthropocene Era — 25
14. Chapter 14: The Quest for Knowledge and Understanding — 27
15. Chapter 15: The Future of Human Progress — 29

1

Chapter 1: The Dawn of Civilization

In the mists of prehistory, humankind transitioned from nomadic tribes to settled agricultural communities. This monumental shift, often referred to as the Neolithic Revolution, was the bedrock of civilization. As people began to cultivate the land and domesticate animals, they formed stable societies that fostered the development of culture, language, and social structures. This newfound stability allowed for the accumulation of surplus food, which in turn supported larger populations and the emergence of complex societies.

The earliest known civilizations sprang up along fertile river valleys such as the Tigris and Euphrates, the Nile, and the Indus. These riverine environments provided the necessary resources for sustained agricultural output, facilitating the rise of urban centers. Mesopotamia, ancient Egypt, and the Indus Valley are prime examples of early advanced civilizations that thrived due to their innovative approaches to agriculture, trade, and governance. These societies laid the groundwork for subsequent human progress by pioneering writing systems, legal codes, and monumental architecture.

As civilizations flourished, they developed intricate social hierarchies and political structures. The concentration of power in the hands of ruling elites, often legitimized by religious or ideological means, allowed for the coordinated effort of large populations in projects such as irrigation, construction, and warfare. The specialization of labor, another hallmark of civilization, led to the creation of various professions and the advancement of technology. Artisans, scribes, and priests played pivotal roles in shaping the cultural and intellectual life of their societies.

The interconnections between early civilizations set the stage for the exchange of ideas, goods, and technologies. Trade routes crisscrossed the ancient world, linking distant regions and fostering a spirit of curiosity and innovation. Through these exchanges, civilizations learned from one another, adapting and enhancing their own practices. This dynamic interplay of influence and adaptation is a testament to the resilience and ingenuity of human societies, setting the stage for the continued march of progress.

2

Chapter 2: The Age of Empires

The rise of empires marked a new phase in the evolution of human societies. As powerful states expanded their territories through conquest and diplomacy, they brought diverse cultures and peoples under their control. This process of empire-building had profound effects on the political, economic, and cultural landscapes of the ancient world. The Persian, Mauryan, and Roman Empires are notable examples of expansive states that shaped the course of history through their governance, infrastructure, and cultural policies.

Empires often relied on a combination of military prowess and administrative acumen to maintain their dominance. The Persian Empire, for instance, utilized a sophisticated network of roads and communication systems to govern its vast territories. The Roman Empire, on the other hand, is renowned for its legal innovations, engineering feats, and cultural assimilation policies. By integrating conquered peoples into their administrative and military systems, empires were able to harness the resources and talents of diverse populations.

The economic impact of empires was equally significant. By creating large, interconnected markets, empires facilitated the flow of goods, wealth, and ideas across vast distances. Trade networks, such as the Silk Road, connected the East and West, enabling the exchange of luxury goods, technological innovations, and cultural practices. These commercial exchanges not only enriched the economies of the empires but also promoted cross-cultural interactions that spurred intellectual and artistic achievements.

The cultural legacy of empires is perhaps their most enduring contribution to human civilization. By promoting the diffusion of languages, religions, and artistic traditions, empires helped to create a shared cultural heritage that transcended regional and ethnic boundaries. The spread of Hellenistic culture under Alexander the Great, the dissemination of Buddhism under Ashoka, and the Romanization of Europe are all examples of how empires shaped the cultural and intellectual landscape of the ancient world. Through these processes, empires laid the foundation for the global civilization we inhabit today.

3

Chapter 3: The Middle Ages

The collapse of the Western Roman Empire in the 5th century CE ushered in a period of political fragmentation and social transformation in Europe. This era, often referred to as the Middle Ages, saw the rise of feudalism, the spread of Christianity, and the emergence of powerful kingdoms and city-states. While commonly perceived as a time of stagnation and decline, the Middle Ages were in fact a period of significant innovation and adaptation that laid the groundwork for the Renaissance and the modern world.

Feudalism, the dominant social and economic system of the Middle Ages, was characterized by a hierarchical structure of landholding and mutual obligations. Lords granted land to vassals in exchange for military service, while peasants, or serfs, worked the land in return for protection and sustenance. This system provided a measure of stability and order in a fragmented political landscape, allowing for the gradual recovery of economic and social life. The manorial system, with its focus on self-sufficient estates, played a crucial role in the agricultural productivity and local governance of medieval Europe.

The spread of Christianity during the Middle Ages had a profound impact on European society. The Church emerged as a powerful institution, influencing all aspects of life from politics to education to morality. Monasticism, the practice of communal living under religious vows, became a significant force in the preservation and dissemination of knowledge. Monasteries served as centers of learning, where ancient texts were copied and studied, and new ideas were developed. The intellectual and cultural achievements of the medieval Church laid the foundation for the scholasticism and humanism that would later flourish during the Renaissance.

The Middle Ages were also a time of remarkable technological and scientific advancements. The invention of the heavy plow, the water mill, and the three-field system of crop rotation greatly improved agricultural productivity. Innovations in architecture, such as the development of the Gothic style, led to the construction of awe-inspiring cathedrals and castles. The growth of towns and the rise of a merchant class facilitated the exchange of goods and ideas, fostering a spirit of exploration and innovation. The medieval period, far from being a dark age, was a time of dynamic change and progress that set the stage for the transformative developments of the Renaissance.

4

Chapter 4: The Renaissance

The Renaissance, spanning roughly the 14th to the 17th century, was a period of profound cultural, intellectual, and artistic flourishing in Europe. Characterized by a renewed interest in classical antiquity and a fervent spirit of inquiry, the Renaissance marked a departure from the medieval worldview and laid the foundations for the modern era. This period saw the rise of humanism, a movement that emphasized the value of human potential and the pursuit of knowledge, and produced some of the most celebrated works of art and literature in history.

At the heart of the Renaissance was the revival of classical learning. Scholars, known as humanists, sought to recover and study the texts of ancient Greece and Rome, believing that these works contained timeless wisdom and insights. The invention of the printing press by Johannes Gutenberg in the mid-15th century revolutionized the dissemination of knowledge, making books more accessible and affordable. This technological advancement facilitated the spread of Renaissance ideas across Europe, sparking an intellectual and cultural awakening.

The Renaissance also witnessed extraordinary achievements in the visual arts. Artists such as Leonardo da Vinci, Michelangelo, and Raphael pushed the boundaries of artistic expression, creating masterpieces that continue to inspire and captivate audiences today. The use of perspective, chiaroscuro, and anatomical accuracy transformed the representation of the human form and the natural world. Patronage from wealthy individuals and institutions, including the Medici family and the Catholic Church, played a crucial role in supporting the arts and fostering a culture of creativity and innovation.

In addition to its artistic and intellectual achievements, the Renaissance was a time of significant scientific and technological advancements. Figures such as Nicolaus Copernicus, Galileo Galilei, and Johannes Kepler challenged the geocentric model of the universe and laid the groundwork for modern astronomy. The study of anatomy, medicine, and engineering advanced through the work of pioneers like Andreas Vesalius and Leonardo da Vinci. The spirit of curiosity and experimentation that defined the Renaissance paved the way for the Scientific Revolution and the profound transformations of the modern era.

5

Chapter 5: The Age of Exploration

The Age of Exploration, which began in the 15th century, was a period of unprecedented global expansion and discovery. Driven by the desire for wealth, knowledge, and new trade routes, European explorers set out to chart unknown territories and establish overseas empires. This era of exploration had far-reaching consequences, reshaping the political, economic, and cultural landscapes of the world and paving the way for the modern globalized society.

The Portuguese and Spanish were at the forefront of this age of exploration. Navigators such as Christopher Columbus, Vasco da Gama, and Ferdinand Magellan embarked on daring voyages that expanded the boundaries of the known world. The discovery of the Americas, the sea route to India, and the circumnavigation of the globe opened new avenues for trade and conquest. These expeditions were fueled by advancements in navigation, shipbuilding, and cartography, which enabled mariners to venture further and with greater accuracy than ever before.

The establishment of overseas colonies and trade networks had profound economic implications. The influx of precious metals and exotic goods from the Americas and Asia enriched European economies and stimulated the growth of commerce and industry. The Columbian Exchange, the widespread transfer of plants, animals, and diseases between the Old and New Worlds, had transformative effects on agriculture, diets, and populations. The rise of global trade also led to the formation of powerful commercial enterprises, such as the Dutch East India Company and the British East India Company, which played significant roles in shaping the course of history.

The Age of Exploration also had significant cultural and intellectual impacts. The encounter with diverse peoples and cultures challenged European perceptions of the world and sparked a spirit of curiosity and inquiry. The writings and observations of explorers, missionaries, and traders provided new insights into the natural world, geography, and ethnography. The Age of Exploration also had significant cultural and intellectual impacts. The encounter with diverse peoples and cultures challenged European perceptions of the world and sparked a spirit of curiosity and inquiry. The writings and observations of explorers, missionaries, and traders provided new insights into the natural world, geography, and ethnography. The age of exploration was not without its darker aspects, however. The exploitation and subjugation of indigenous peoples, the transatlantic slave trade, and the environmental consequences of colonization left a legacy of suffering and injustice that continues to resonate today.

Despite these challenges, the Age of Exploration remains a pivotal chapter in human history. It marked the beginning of a truly interconnected world, where the exchange of ideas, goods, and cultures could occur on an unprecedented scale. The spirit of exploration and discovery that characterized this era continues to inspire and drive human progress.

6

Chapter 6: The Scientific Revolution

The Scientific Revolution, spanning roughly the 16th to the 18th centuries, was a period of dramatic transformation in the way humans understood the natural world. Driven by a spirit of inquiry and skepticism, scientists began to challenge long-held beliefs and develop new theories based on observation, experimentation, and mathematical reasoning. This period saw the emergence of the modern scientific method and laid the foundations for the technological advancements that have shaped the modern world.

Key figures of the Scientific Revolution, such as Copernicus, Galileo, Newton, and Kepler, made groundbreaking contributions to our understanding of the universe. Copernicus's heliocentric model of the solar system challenged the geocentric view that had dominated for centuries, while Galileo's observations with the telescope provided compelling evidence for this new paradigm. Newton's laws of motion and universal gravitation unified the study of physics, while Kepler's laws of planetary motion described the elliptical orbits of planets.

The impact of the Scientific Revolution extended beyond the realm of natural philosophy. The development of new instruments, such as the microscope and the barometer, opened up new fields of study and allowed scientists to explore previously unseen phenomena. The increasing emphasis on empirical evidence and rational inquiry also influenced other areas of intellectual life, including philosophy, political theory, and economics. Thinkers such as Descartes, Locke, and Smith applied the principles of the scientific method to their respective fields, laying the groundwork for the Enlightenment and the modern intellectual landscape.

The Scientific Revolution also had profound social and cultural implications. The dissemination of scientific knowledge through books, journals, and societies such as the Royal Society fostered a culture of intellectual exchange and collaboration. The growing acceptance of scientific ideas challenged traditional authority and promoted a spirit of critical inquiry and innovation. The legacy of the Scientific Revolution is evident in the continued pursuit of knowledge and the technological advancements that define the modern era.

7

Chapter 7: The Enlightenment

The Enlightenment, which flourished in the 18th century, was an intellectual and cultural movement that emphasized reason, individualism, and human rights. Building on the advancements of the Scientific Revolution, Enlightenment thinkers sought to apply rational inquiry to all aspects of human life, from politics and economics to education and ethics. This period of intellectual ferment produced some of the most influential ideas and works in Western history and laid the foundations for modern democratic and liberal thought.

Central to the Enlightenment was the belief in the power of reason to improve the human condition. Philosophers such as Voltaire, Rousseau, and Kant argued that human beings could achieve progress through the application of reason and the pursuit of knowledge. They challenged traditional authority and advocated for individual rights, equality, and freedom of thought and expression. The principles of the Enlightenment inspired revolutions and reforms that transformed the political landscape of the Western world.

The Enlightenment also had a profound impact on education and the dissemination of knowledge. The establishment of academies, libraries, and universities promoted the exchange of ideas and the development of new fields of study. The publication of encyclopedias and other reference works made knowledge more accessible and fostered a culture of intellectual curiosity and inquiry. The ideals of the Enlightenment influenced the development of public education systems and the promotion of literacy and learning.

The cultural achievements of the Enlightenment were equally significant. The period saw a flourishing of the arts, literature, and music, with figures such as Mozart, Goethe, and Hogarth making lasting contributions to their respective fields. The emphasis on reason and individual expression fostered new artistic and literary forms, from the novel to the symphony. The Enlightenment's legacy of intellectual curiosity, critical inquiry, and cultural innovation continues to shape our world today.

8

Chapter 8: The Industrial Revolution

The Industrial Revolution, which began in the late 18th century, was a period of profound economic and technological change that transformed human society. Driven by advancements in machinery, energy production, and manufacturing techniques, the Industrial Revolution ushered in an era of unprecedented productivity, urbanization, and social change. This period marked a fundamental shift in the way goods were produced and consumed, laying the foundations for the modern industrial economy.

At the heart of the Industrial Revolution was the development of new technologies that revolutionized manufacturing and transportation. The invention of the steam engine by James Watt, the mechanization of textile production, and the development of iron and steel production processes were key innovations that powered industrial growth. The construction of railways and canals facilitated the movement of goods and people, creating new markets and opportunities for trade and commerce.

The impact of the Industrial Revolution on society was profound. The rise of factories and urban centers led to significant demographic changes, as people moved from rural areas to cities in search of employment. The growth of industrial capitalism created new social classes, with industrialists and entrepreneurs amassing great wealth and influence. The working conditions in factories, however, were often harsh and exploitative, leading to calls for labor reform and the rise of trade unions and social movements.

The Industrial Revolution also had significant cultural and intellectual implications. The rapid pace of technological change and economic growth inspired a sense of optimism and progress, but also raised concerns about the social and environmental consequences of industrialization. Writers, artists, and thinkers grappled with the tensions and contradictions of the industrial age, exploring themes of alienation, inequality, and the impact of technology on human life. The Industrial Revolution set the stage for the modern world, shaping the economic, social, and cultural landscapes we inhabit today.

9

Chapter 9: The Modern Era

The Modern Era, spanning from the late 19th century to the present, has been marked by rapid technological, social, and political changes that have transformed human society. The period has seen the rise of new ideologies, the impact of global conflicts, and the development of technologies that have revolutionized the way we live, work, and communicate. The Modern Era has been characterized by both unprecedented progress and profound challenges, as humanity navigates the complexities of an interconnected world.

One of the defining features of the Modern Era has been the rise of new ideologies and political movements. The late 19th and early 20th centuries saw the emergence of socialism, communism, and fascism, as well as the growth of democratic and nationalist movements. These ideologies shaped the course of global conflicts, from the World Wars to the Cold War, and influenced the political landscape of the 20th century. The struggle for human rights, decolonization, and civil rights also marked this period, as marginalized groups fought for equality and justice.

Technological advancements have been a driving force of the Modern Era. The development of electricity, automobiles, and airplanes transformed transportation and communication, shrinking distances and connecting people across the globe. The advent of computers and the internet revolutionized information and communication, creating a digital age that has reshaped every aspect of human life. Advances in medicine, science, and engineering have improved health, extended lifespans, and expanded our understanding of the natural world.

The Modern Era has also been marked by profound social and cultural changes. The rise of mass media, popular culture, and consumerism has created new forms of expression and identity. The growth of education and the spread of literacy have empowered individuals and communities, fostering a culture of innovation and creativity. However, the period has also witnessed significant challenges, including environmental degradation, economic inequality, and geopolitical tensions. As humanity faces the uncertainties of the future, the lessons and achievements of the Modern Era continue to shape our world.

10

Chapter 10: The Digital Age

The Digital Age, which began in the late 20th century, has been characterized by the rapid development and adoption of digital technologies that have transformed every aspect of human life. The rise of the internet, smartphones, and social media has created a connected world where information flows freely and instantaneously. The Digital Age has ushered in a new era of communication, commerce, and innovation, but also presents unique challenges and ethical dilemmas.

At the heart of the Digital Age is the internet, a global network that has revolutionized the way we access and share information. The development of the World Wide Web in the early 1990s and the subsequent explosion of online content have created an unprecedented wealth of knowledge and resources. Social media platforms have transformed the way we connect and communicate, enabling people to share their lives, ideas, and experiences with a global audience. The rise of e-commerce has reshaped the retail landscape, making it possible to buy and sell goods and services from anywhere in the world.

The impact of digital technologies on the economy has been profound. The growth of the tech industry has created new opportunities for innovation and entrepreneurship, driving economic growth and job creation. The rise of the gig economy and remote work has transformed traditional employment models, offering flexibility and autonomy but also raising concerns about job security and workers' rights. The digital revolution has also spurred advancements in artificial intelligence, robotics, and automation, with implications for the future of work and society.

The Digital Age has also raised important ethical and social questions. The widespread use of digital technologies has brought issues of privacy, security, and digital literacy to the forefront. The spread of misinformation and the impact of social media on mental health and social cohesion are pressing concerns that require thoughtful solutions. As society navigates the complexities of the digital landscape, there is a need for policies and practices that promote responsible and equitable use of technology.

Despite these challenges, the Digital Age has brought about remarkable advancements and opportunities. The democratization of information and the ability to connect and collaborate across borders have empowered individuals and communities in unprecedented ways. The potential for innovation and positive change in areas such as education, healthcare, and environmental sustainability is immense. As we continue to embrace and shape the digital future, the values of creativity, inclusivity, and ethical responsibility will be essential in harnessing the full potential of this transformative era.

11

Chapter 11: The Globalized World

The late 20th and early 21st centuries have witnessed the rise of globalization, a process characterized by the increasing interconnectedness and interdependence of countries and cultures. Driven by advances in communication, transportation, and trade, globalization has reshaped the economic, political, and cultural landscapes of the world. While it has brought about significant opportunities for growth and development, it has also posed challenges and sparked debates about inequality, cultural identity, and sustainability.

Globalization has facilitated the flow of goods, services, and capital across borders, creating a global marketplace where businesses and consumers can access products and resources from around the world. The expansion of international trade and investment has contributed to economic growth and poverty reduction in many countries. The rise of multinational corporations and global supply chains has transformed industries and created new opportunities for innovation and collaboration.

The cultural impact of globalization is equally profound. The exchange of ideas, traditions, and artistic expressions has enriched societies and fostered a greater appreciation for diversity. The proliferation of media and technology has enabled the spread of cultural products and trends, creating a global cultural landscape that is both dynamic and interconnected. However, the rapid pace of cultural exchange has also raised concerns about the erosion of local cultures and the dominance of certain cultural forms.

Globalization has also highlighted the need for international cooperation and governance. Global challenges such as climate change, pandemics, and economic inequality require collaborative efforts and coordinated responses. International organizations, treaties, and agreements play a crucial role in addressing these issues and promoting sustainable development. As the world becomes increasingly interconnected, the principles of equity, justice, and solidarity will be essential in navigating the complexities of globalization.

12

Chapter 12: The Knowledge Economy

The transition to a knowledge economy, characterized by the central role of information, innovation, and intellectual capital, has been a defining feature of the late 20th and early 21st centuries. In this new economic paradigm, the creation, dissemination, and application of knowledge drive growth and development, transforming industries and reshaping the labor market. The knowledge economy has profound implications for education, employment, and social equity, presenting both opportunities and challenges.

At the heart of the knowledge economy is the increasing importance of information and communication technologies (ICTs). The rapid development and adoption of digital tools and platforms have revolutionized the way we produce, share, and consume information. The rise of the internet, cloud computing, and artificial intelligence has created new opportunities for innovation and entrepreneurship, enabling individuals and organizations to leverage knowledge and data in novel ways.

The knowledge economy has also transformed the nature of work and employment. The demand for high-skilled workers with expertise in technology, science, and creative fields has increased, while traditional manufacturing and low-skilled jobs have declined. This shift has led to the growth of knowledge-intensive industries such as finance, healthcare, and information services. However, the changing labor market has also raised concerns about job displacement, skills gaps, and income inequality, highlighting the need for policies that promote education, training, and social protection.

Education and lifelong learning are critical to success in the knowledge economy. The emphasis on skills development, critical thinking, and digital literacy has reshaped educational systems and curricula. The rise of online learning platforms and digital resources has made education more accessible and flexible, enabling individuals to acquire new skills and knowledge throughout their lives. The knowledge economy underscores the importance of investing in human capital and fostering a culture of innovation and continuous learning.

13

Chapter 13: The Anthropocene Era

The Anthropocene, a term used to describe the current geological epoch in which human activity has become the dominant influence on the environment, has profound implications for the future of civilization. The impact of human actions on the planet's ecosystems, climate, and biodiversity has reached unprecedented levels, raising urgent questions about sustainability, resilience, and stewardship. The Anthropocene challenges humanity to reconsider its relationship with the natural world and chart a path toward a more sustainable and equitable future.

One of the defining features of the Anthropocene is the impact of human activity on the Earth's climate. The burning of fossil fuels, deforestation, and industrial processes have led to a significant increase in greenhouse gas emissions, causing global warming and climate change. The consequences of climate change, including rising sea levels, extreme weather events, and disruptions to ecosystems, pose significant risks to human societies and the natural world. Addressing these challenges requires urgent and coordinated action to reduce emissions, promote renewable energy, and build resilience to climate impacts.

The Anthropocene also highlights the loss of biodiversity and the degradation of ecosystems. Human activities such as habitat destruction, pollution, and overexploitation of resources have led to a dramatic decline in wildlife populations and the disruption of ecological processes. The preservation and restoration of biodiversity are critical to maintaining the health and functioning of ecosystems, which provide essential services such as clean air, water, and food. Conservation efforts, sustainable resource management, and the protection of natural habitats are essential to safeguarding the planet's ecological integrity.

The concept of the Anthropocene also raises important ethical and philosophical questions about humanity's role and responsibility in shaping the future of the planet. The recognition of humans as a geological force challenges traditional notions of the separation between nature and culture and calls for a more integrated and holistic approach to addressing environmental issues. The principles of sustainability, justice, and intergenerational equity are central to this new paradigm, emphasizing the need to balance human well-being with the health of the planet.

14

Chapter 14: The Quest for Knowledge and Understanding

The pursuit of knowledge and understanding has been a driving force throughout human history, shaping the course of civilization and fostering progress in diverse fields. From the earliest myths and philosophies to the latest scientific discoveries and technological innovations, the quest for knowledge reflects humanity's innate curiosity and desire to make sense of the world. This chapter explores the evolution of human thought and the enduring importance of intellectual inquiry in shaping our present and future.

Ancient civilizations made significant contributions to the development of knowledge and philosophy. The thinkers of ancient Greece, China, and India laid the foundations for fields such as mathematics, astronomy, ethics, and metaphysics. Their inquiries into the nature of reality, the human condition, and the cosmos have had a lasting impact on the development of intellectual traditions and continue to inspire contemporary thought.

The Scientific Revolution and the Enlightenment marked significant milestones in the quest for knowledge, transforming the way humans understood and interacted with the world. The development of the scientific method, the emphasis on empirical evidence, and the application of reason and critical thinking paved the way for modern science and technology.

The contributions of scientists, philosophers, and scholars during these periods laid the groundwork for the rapid advancements and discoveries that characterize the modern era.

In the contemporary world, the pursuit of knowledge continues to drive innovation and progress in diverse fields. The integration of disciplines such as biology, physics, computer science, and social sciences has led to groundbreaking discoveries and transformative technologies. The exploration of new frontiers, from space to the depths of the ocean to the intricacies of the human brain, reflects humanity's enduring curiosity and determination to expand the boundaries of understanding.

15

Chapter 15: The Future of Human Progress

As we look to the future, the trajectory of human progress is shaped by a complex interplay of technological advancements, social dynamics, and philosophical considerations. The challenges and opportunities of the 21st century demand innovative solutions, ethical foresight, and a commitment to the well-being of both people and the planet. This final chapter explores the potential paths forward and the principles that can guide humanity toward a more equitable, sustainable, and enlightened future.

Technological innovation will continue to be a driving force in shaping the future. Advances in fields such as artificial intelligence, biotechnology, and renewable energy hold the promise of addressing pressing global challenges and improving the quality of life. However, the responsible development and deployment of these technologies require careful consideration of their ethical implications and potential impacts on society. The principles of transparency, accountability, and inclusivity will be essential in guiding the ethical governance of emerging technologies.

Social progress and equity are central to the future of human civilization. The pursuit of justice, equality, and human rights remains a fundamental goal, as societies work to address issues of poverty, discrimination, and inequality. The empowerment of marginalized groups, the promotion of inclusive and participatory governance, and the protection of individual freedoms are crucial to building resilient and cohesive communities. Education, healthcare, and social protection are key areas where investments can create lasting positive change.

Environmental sustainability is paramount to the future of human progress. The preservation of the planet's ecosystems, the mitigation of climate change, and the sustainable management of natural resources are essential to ensuring the health and well-being of current and future generations. The principles of stewardship, intergenerational equity, and ecological resilience provide a framework for sustainable development that balances human needs with the protection of the natural world.

Ultimately, the future of human progress is shaped by the choices and actions of individuals, communities, and societies. The values of curiosity, creativity, compassion, and ethical responsibility will be essential in navigating the complexities of the 21st century and beyond. As humanity continues its journey, the clockwork of civilization, driven by the interplay of history, technology, and philosophy

The Clockwork of Civilization: How History, Technology, and Philosophy Shape Human Progress

In "The Clockwork of Civilization," readers embark on an enlightening journey through the pivotal moments and forces that have shaped human history. Spanning from the dawn of civilization to the digital age, this book delves into the intricate interplay of history, technology, and philosophy that drives human progress.

Each chapter provides a detailed exploration of significant eras and phenomena, from the rise of ancient empires and the transformative power of the Renaissance, to the scientific breakthroughs of the Enlightenment and the far-reaching impacts of globalization and the knowledge economy. The book examines the profound consequences of human actions on the environment in the Anthropocene era and contemplates the future of human progress in an increasingly complex world.

With a focus on the interconnectedness of human endeavors, "The Clockwork of Civilization" highlights the resilience, curiosity, and ingenuity that

CHAPTER 15: THE FUTURE OF HUMAN PROGRESS

define our species. It invites readers to reflect on the lessons of the past and consider the ethical responsibilities that come with shaping the future. This book is an engaging and insightful exploration of the forces that have propelled humanity forward, offering a comprehensive understanding of the clockwork mechanisms that underpin our civilization.

www.ingramcontent.com/pod-product-compliance
Lightning Source LLC
LaVergne TN
LVHW020502080526
838202LV00057B/6119